Once there lived two friends in a village. Their names were Harry and Sam.

Harry was a very rich man, whereas Sam was very poor. Harry was very cunning and looking

for an opportunity to capture all his friend's property.

One day on the occasion of his daughter's marriage, Sam borrowed some money from Harry. He told Harry that he would repay the loan bit by bit later as he was heavily in debt due to the marriage.

Harry saw through this opportunity. After some days, he made an evil plan to capture Sam's property. He called Sam and asked him to repay the loan immediately. Sam was stunned to hear this. He requested Harry to give him some more time.

He promised his friend that even though he was a poor man, he would pay every rupee of his money. But Harry was having some other plans in his mind. He insisted to get his money back immediately. He knew that Sam was now

in his trap and he should try to get hold of his property either by hook or by crook.

Finally, Harry said, "If you are an honest man, then come with me to the king's court and sign the papers saying that you have mortgaged your house to me against the loan."

Sam was very disappointed to hear this.

He never expected such a behaviour from his best friend.
He tried to convince Harry, "Why do you want to go to the court? Believe me, I don't wish to cheat you. I will pay the loan as early as possible."
But Harry was in no mood to listen. He insisted that Sam should come with him to the court and

sign the papers in the presence of the judge. Now Sam realised the evil intentions of his friend. He thought for a moment and said, "I don't have a horse to ride to the court. I don't have good clothes to wear. I don't have shoes to wear. So how can I come with you?"

Harry instantly told Sam that he would give him all the things he wanted, a horse, clothes and a pair of shoes. When Harry gave him all these

things, he wore them, and mounting on Harry's horse he rode to the court.

After some time, Sam's name was called out in the court. He appeared before the judge and appealed, "My Lord, my friend, Harry, says that everything that belongs to me, is his.

He is my neighbour and always quarrels with me. I wish to ask my friend some questions in your presence."

The judge then called Harry and ordered him to answer the questions of Sam. Sam first asked, “Whom does the horse, which I rode to the court, belong to?” Harry replied, “It belongs to me.”

“Whom do the clothes, I wear, belong to?” asked

Sam. "The clothes belong to me, " replied Harry. Finally Sam asked, "Whom do the shoes, on my feet, belong to?" "They too belong to me," shouted Harry in an irritating voice.

"The horse, the clothes and the shoes are all

mine," said Harry. When the people in the court heard this, they started laughing loudly. They thought that Harry had gone crazy. He mistook Sam's belongings as his own.

The judge declared that Harry had become mad and dismissed the case. He told that all of Sam's possessions belong to him only.

Once upon a time, a poor Brahmin lived in a village. His financial condition was very bad. He did not have even proper clothes to wear and enough food to eat. The Brahmin's wife was very much upset.

She wished to lead a comfortable life. She started telling her husband to go to the neighbouring village, find some job and earn more money.

The Brahmin finally agreed and started his journey to the neighbouring village. He had to pass through a forest.

While he was walking through the forest, he heard some noise coming from a well. He went near it and saw a tiger, a monkey, a snake, and a man inside it. The tiger first spoke to the Brahmin, "O noble sir, kindly help me come out of this well." The Brahmin replied, "I don't

trust you. You may kill me if you come out." But the tiger convinced him that he would not harm him. When the Brahmin pulled the tiger out of the well, the tiger said, "I live in a den in that hill. When you find time, please pay me a visit. I want to repay for your kindness."

Then the monkey requested the Brahmin to help him come out of the well. The Brahmin also pulled out the monkey out of the well. The monkey too invited the Brahmin to visit him whenever he wished. In this way the other two, the snake and the man, also came out and thanked the Brahmin for saving their lives.

The Brahmin continued his journey. He went to different villages and earned enough money. He now decided to return home and see his family. While returning, he had to pass through the same forest. He thought of the invitation of the tiger and the monkey. First, he went to the monkey who welcomed the Brahmin and offered him sweet fruits to eat. Next the Brahmin

went to the tiger's den. The tiger offered the Brahmin some ornaments. He said, "I killed a prince who came by this way. These ornaments belonged to me. Now you can keep them." The Brahmin was very happy.

He decided to sell the gold ornaments to the goldsmith, whom the Brahmin saved from the well. He went to him and showed the gold ornaments. He requested the goldsmith,"I want you to sell these ornaments for me."

The goldsmith saw the ornaments and immediately recognised them as the ones he had made for the prince. He asked the Brahmin

to wait for some time. In the meantime, the goldsmith ran to the king's palace and told him about the man and showed the ornaments.

The king instantly recognised ornaments as the ones that belonged to his dead son. He immediately ordered his soldiers, "Go and catch hold of the man in the shop of the goldsmith. He is the one who has killed my son. Put him in the prison."

Within no time, the Brahmin was in the prison. Then he remembered the snake. The snake immediately came there and asked what he could do for him. The Brahmin requested him to help him out of the prison. The snake said to the Brahmin, "I will definitely help you. I will bite the queen. Only your touch will cure her.

Then the king will set you free." Saying this the snake went to the queen and bit her. The queen instantly became unconscious.

The physicians of the kingdom were not able to cure her. The king was terribly worried about her life. He sent out a proclamation that the person who could revive the queen would be richly rewarded. The Brahmin heard this. He told the guards that he could cure the queen.

The Brahmin was taken to the king. As soon as the Brahmin touched the queen, she opened her eyes. The king was very happy. He immediately set the Brahmin free. He asked him how his son's ornaments fell into his hands.

The Brahmin told him all the things that had happened.

The king was fully convinced with the Brahmin's story. He asked his soldiers to arrest the goldsmith. He made the Brahmin a minister in his court. He also honoured the Brahmin with some precious gifts.